Portfolio management

Beginner`s guide to construct, understand and manage portfolio investment

By

M. Imran Ahsan

Preface

Thank you for trusting us. This is another book of investment series for the investors. We have used the same preciseness yet comprehensibility in preparing this book. It covers all necessary tools required for the Portfolio Management. Usually investors struggle with evaluation and management. This book intends to solve that problem, nevertheless this is most affordable with quality study material. This book is prepared very carefully to make everybody feel happy about the whole course because they can easily grasp it now. So yes you should study and once again thanks for all the support and trust.

I am looking forward to come up with more books. Love you all the investors and may you succeed in your goals. Please don't hesitate to contact me about any issue.

M. Imran Ahsan

Ch.imranahsen@gmail.com

Whats app# 00923465006818

Contents

Portfolio Management: An Overview

Portfolio approach and investment

Portfolio means collection of different investments by individual investors or institutions in order to reduce investment risk. Different investments include holding stocks of different companies, bonds, real estate etc. The process of holding different types of investment at same time is called diversification.

When an investor holds a single security, she is not diversifying her investment. It means if the security price fall, all of her investment will go down. On the other hand holding a lot of securities reduce risk because some securities will fall while others will rise with the passage of time. There is a famous quote "Do not put all your eggs into a single basket".

An investor must try to hold the securities with highest negative correlation. "-1" is the ideal correlation for portfolio diversification. If two securities have -1 correlation, it means they move in opposite direction and it's a 100 % hedge against risk. Investors should focus on the correlation between the securities within portfolio because the correlation can change over time.

Always remember portfolio diversification is hedge against market risk in normal market conditions. In an era of market turmoil, generally all securities prices fall. This phenomenon is called contagion (for example (2008 crisis).

Steps in the portfolio management process

There are three steps in portfolio management process;

1. Planning
2. Execution
3. Feedback

1. **Planning:** In this step we analyze client's investment goal, time horizon, risk tolerance, liquidity needs, tax and other obligations and other circumstances which can affect her investment. After the analysis we write IPS (Investment policy statement). IPS

contains investment objectives, constraints and a related benchmark to compare portfolio`s performance. This statement can be and should be updated as soon as investor`s circumstances change.

2. **Execution:** In this step we do following; Asset allocation, security analysis and construct portfolio according to IPS. It means we (as an analyst) analyze risk and return characteristics of different securities and allocate the client's funds and develop a portfolio. The resultant portfolio must match the risk tolerance and return goals of the investor.

   The analyst use top-down analysis for the asset allocation. It may include over all macroeconomic conditions like GDP growth rate, inflation rate, interest rate etc. After that, bottom-up analysis is done by examining attractive and under-valuated securities. We can develop portfolio containing stocks, fixed income private and government securities.

3. **Feedback:** Once the portfolio is developed, it must be monitored and rebalanced after intervals or whenever

the investor`s or overall macroeconomic
circumstances changes. For example if a
security`s risk characteristics increases
we should eliminate and replace it with
another security with less risk
characteristic. The portfolio must be
monitored evaluated with respect to
benchmark and reported to client.

Types of investors and distinctive characteristics

The need and characteristics of every investor
can vary but we can group them into two
broad categories: the individual investors and
institutional investors.

1. **Individual Investors:** Individual
   investors can have short term or long
   term goals. For example plan to buy a
   house or children's education can be a
   short term goal while plan for retirement
   pension is a long term goal. Some
   individual investors look for fixed income
   generating opportunities while others
   want capital appreciation and or
   deferment of taxes. Some individual
   investors are retail investors while others
   can be "high-net-worth investors. Their
   investment goals can also depend on
   their financial position, employment and

other obligations so does their risk tolerance.

2. **Institutional Investors:** Institutional investors can also have long term and or short term investment goals. Usually institutional investors are the major participants in financial market. Institutional investors can be following;

Banks: Usually the banks have short term investment goals. They want to earn extra on excessive reserves. They usually invest in liquid assets like money market instruments so they can quickly withdraw funds to fulfill depositors' claims.

Insurance companies: Insurance companies sell insurance products and receive premiums. They need to invest so that they have sufficient funds to fulfill insurance claims. Some insurance companies like life- insurance have long term objectives while property and loss insurance companies have shorter time horizons.

Investment companies: Investment companies need to invest a pool of funds in different securities in order to earn for their financers. Time horizon of different investment companies differ with respect to their investment goals. Some companies use conservative approach to save principal amount while earning. Some companies use aggressive investment approach to earn extra.

Endowment funds: Endowment funds can invest in a way to maintain principal amount (inflation adjusted) while earning a rate of return to fund some ongoing projects like educational and or general welfare projects. Usually the time horizon of these funds is longer.

Foundations: Foundations are charitable institutions which are established for the welfare of a particular region, people or to support other welfare projects like creating a vaccine for a specific disease. The investment time horizon of a foundation can be the same as endowment fund because it also has to save original amount (inflation adjusted) while funding some ongoing project. Usually the time horizon of foundations is longer.

Sovereign investment fund: It is the investment company owned by government. These funds invest excessive government funds to earn and to maintain principal amount (inflation adjusted).

Defined contribution and defined benefit pension plans

Pension: It is the amount of funds collected from employees during their services. These funds are used to support the person after retirement.

The two broad categories of pension plan are defined contribution plan and defined pension plan.

Defined contribution plan: It is a retirement plan in which employer contributes a certain amount of money in each period (i.e. monthly) into employee`s retirement account. The contribution may depend on employee`s contribution, employee`s experience, duration of employee`s services etc. The employee can also contribute same or different amount. The firm provides no promises about the future value of the plan. The money is invested and it can earn positive or negative earnings. The investment decisions are left to employee. The employee bears all the risks involved linked to investment.

Defined benefit plan: It is a retirement plan in which the employer assumes risk of future value of the plan. The employer promises to pay certain periodic payments to employee in future (after retirement). In this plan the employer contributes certain amount (the employee may or may not contribute) into fund. The employer generally sends the amount to an institution which is specialized for investment. The employer makes sure a certain future value of the fund. The retirement benefits usually depend on employee`s years of service, or the compensations at retirement. For example, an employee who is to be entitled 3% of her salary (0f $200000) and served for 30 years may get

200000 x 30 x 2% = $120000

Asset management industry

Asset management industry is a collection of all firms who deal with investment assets.

Asset management industry can include "buy-side and sell-side firms, Active or passive managers, Traditional or alternative form of investment firms etc.

Buy side vs sell side: Usually when we talk about asset management firms, we mean buy-side firms. These firms buy investment product for their clients and help them to achieve their financial goals.

Buy-side can include retail investors, high-net-worth investors, institutional investors, mutual funds, private equity funds, pension funds etc. on the other hand sell-side firms include all those firms who sell investment products like commercial and investment banks and brokers.

Active vs passive management firms: Active investment managers try to beat the benchmark and are expected to earn more than passive management firms. Active managers use aggressive strategies to achieve their goal. Passive managers just try to replicate benchmark.

Conventional/traditional vs alternative investment management: Traditional investment means investment in common, preferred stocks and or bonds and to create diversified portfolio.

Alternative investment managers invest directly or indirectly in derivatives, real estate private equity etc. A new trend is being emerged that the conventional investment managers are also taking part in alternative investments to diversify their portfolios.

Latest trends in asset management industry

Lately the investors are moving towards passive investment because the fee is very low and also because the active management is not producing (or at least it seems to) much excessive returns due to highly efficient markets. When the markets are efficient they quickly adjust to new information and there is little room for the profitable transactions.

Different types of modern software are being used to analyze huge amount of data (big data) (using different models and algorithms to predict future more accurately. They analyze the date in a quick way. Managers who use these techniques will be able to predict and exploit any opportunity and can involve in short term trading.

Robo-advisors are digital platforms that provide automated financial services to investors with little or even without human involvement. These advisors are efficient and charge lowest fee.

Pooled investments are the investment vehicles which deal with different investments. These vehicles include mutual funds, exchange traded funds, hedge funds and asset backed securities.

Mutual funds

Mutual funds hold the securities of other companies. The investors can buy the securities of these funds directly from the funds (open end funds) or from existing investors (closed end funds). Buying securities of a mutual fund is an alternative of having a portfolio. This is because the mutual funds hold diversified portfolio of securities. Investors can invest in mutual funds with generally low minimum investment. These funds are evaluated by NAV (net asset value). Net asset value is determined at closing price of underlying securities held by that fund in portfolio.

Open-end mutual fund: As the name shows, these funds always accept new funds from investors. The investors can purchase units of these mutual funds at NAV at the time of investment. The investors can also withdraw their funds at NAV at time of withdrawal minus fee and other charges. The managers of these funds have to continuously search for new securities for new inflow of funds and to manage cash for withdrawals. That's why they charge higher fee usually for withdrawals. Due to continuous inflows and outflows, total numbers of shares of these funds continuously change. Inflow of cash can also create opportunities for open end funds to grow. The dividend income is used to purchase extra units of open end mutual funds (the managers offer existing investors to buy extra units of mutual funds with dividend income).

<u>Closed-end mutual funds:</u> The share of closed-end mutual funds is lower in mutual fund industry. These funds do not accept new inflow of cash. New investor can invest in these funds only when existing shareholder sell her shares. So the total number of shares does not change. Trade of shares does not necessarily at NAV but can be at discount or at premium. Due to no continuous inflow and outflow of cash, managers of these funds can invest according to plan and they do not feel any pressure to search for new securities or to entertain any withdrawal request.

Load vs No-load mutual funds: Load funds charge additional fee for purchase of securities (up-front fee) or redemption fee (at time of redemption of shares) or both. These fees are charged to cover for the cost of buying, cost of holding and or sale costs of securities. On the other hand no load mutual funds do not charge any of these fee but they can charge annual management fee which is generally a percentage of NAV.

Types of mutual funds

Money market mutual funds: As the name suggests, these funds invest in short term securities. They are just like bank deposits with a very little level of extra risk. They can be taxable or tax free. Usually these funds invest in bonds with maturity of less than one year.

Bond market mutual funds: These funds invest in medium to longer term bond market (bonds having maturity of more than one year).

Stock market mutual funds: These are the most popular mutual funds. They invest in stocks. These funds can be actively or passively managed. Actively managed funds charge higher fee because their expected rate of return is higher. The passively managed funds charge lower fee while they try to earn their benchmark rate of return. The taxes are also higher for actively managed funds as there is higher turnover. Stock market funds are also called equity funds.

Hybrid funds: Hybrid or balanced funds invest in money as well as equity market.

Other pooled investments

Exchange traded funds: These are like closed-end funds except two differences. EFTs are usually passively managed while closed-end funds are usually actively managed. Closed-end funds usually trade at discount or at premium from NAV but EFTs are traded at or very close to NAV because of purchase and sales in secondary market. The investors can buy the shares of these funds in secondary market just like any other shares. Investors can receive dividends and can sale their ownership in trading hours in stock exchange only by paying brokerage commission. Investors of ETFs can involve intra-day trading and there is not up-front or redemption fee involved. The minimum investment requirement for EFTs is also very lower than mutual funds.

Commodity exchange traded funds (commodity ETFs): These are the funds that invest in physical commodities or hold derivatives of the commodities. The investors can buy the equity of these funds.

Hedge funds: These are usually limited partnerships in which the mangers are general partners and the qualified investors are limited partners. These funds apply aggressive strategies to beat the market. These funds have two fee structures; management fee and incentive fee. Use of leverage is very common characteristic of these funds.

Hedge funds are actively managed funds. Hedge funds always restrict redemption. There is a lock period before which the funds cannot be withdrawn. Funds providers have to give early notice for the funds to be withdrawn. There is always a redemption fee.
Funds of hedge funds hold the equity of many hedge funds.
Hedge funds trade through prime brokers. Prime brokers provide many services to them like custodial, administrative services, money and securities lending along with the trading services.

Benefits and Risks: Managers of hedge funds are experts and use different strategies to diversify and reduce overall risks. But the element of risk cannot be eliminated and there are risks associated with hedge funds as they are actively managed. Usually the returns of hedge funds are less correlated with other securities but the correlation tends to get higher at time of crisis.

Structure of hedge fund and fee: Hedge funds are also less regulated and less transparent. Hedge funds have two types of fee; management fee and performance fee. The management fee is necessarily to be paid to cover the operational expenditures of fund. It usually ranges from 1 to 4 percent of net assets under management. The performance fee is paid only if the performance exceeds the hurdle rate (the minimum benchmark). The incentive fee can be in between 10 to 50 percent. Some hedge funds use high water mark instead of hurdle rate. In high water mark the losses of previous period are also carried forward to check the performance of the fund.

Hedge fund valuation: The value of a hedge fund is the market value of the securities in portfolio. For liquid securities a conservative approach or average value is used. Conservative approach means we take the market price at which the securities can be immediately sold. For example bind price for buying and ask price for sale. In average approach we average the bind and ask prices. For illiquid securities a reduced price of quoted price is used (for bid and ask) to account for the illiquidity. Some funds use NAV.

<u>High water mark:</u> This is another fee structure of hedge funds. In this structure the incentive fee can only be paid if the net gains are crossing the hurdle rate. It means the gains which just offset the previous losses cannot be given incentive fee.

Fund of funds charge another fee structure. They charge another management fee and incentive fee (in excess of original management and performance fee).

The management fee can be calculated as beginning-period-value under management of end of period value of assets under management. The incentive fee can be calculated as net of management fee (assets under management – management fee) or independent of management fee.

Individually managed accounts/ separately managed accounts/wrap accounts: These are for high net worth investors or institutions that have their own investment goals, tax and other financial circumstances. Minimum investment requirement for these accounts is higher than any other pooled investment because these are tailor made investments exclusively for the investors. The investor is the direct owner of all securities purchased unlike mutual funds.

Private equity funds: Private equity funds are private investment vehicles which have two types of partners; General partners and limited partners.

These funds invest in private companies (not publically traded companies) or in the publically traded companies who need funds to go private. Often leverage buyouts (LBOs) are mostly major part of private equity fund portfolios.

These funds are limited partnerships like hedge funds. Committed capital is what the investors provide to the fund. Committed capital may not necessarily invested all at a time but may be draw- down over a period of time as the new investable securities are identified and added into portfolio. This drawdown period is on the discretion of manager.

<u>Fee structure:</u> The fee varies from 1 to 3 percent of committed capital. The incentive or performance fee is typically 20 percent of profit. The managers cannot get performance fee until the original capital is returned to the investors. If in start the fund performs extremely good but in later periods the performance is less than previous periods, the incentive fee may goes beyond 20 percent. If as a whole the investors are not getting 80 percent of the total profit "claw back " provision make the manager to return the excessive performance fee.

Venture capital funds: In venture capital the investment is made in new companies who have great potential to grow if they are financed. Once the company is established it can be sold by IPOs.

PORTFOLIO RISK AND RETURN: PART I

Return measures and their appropriate uses

These are two types of return on a portfolio (or any investment): Dividend/interest income and capital appreciation. Let's have a look at different measures of return. We will move from most simple to most complex one.

Holding period return: It measures total return (dividend or interest plus capital appreciation) in a given period of time. This measure is simple to calculate and can be used for single period.

$$Holding\ Period\ Return = \frac{Dividend\ payments\ +\ Capital\ gain)}{Initial\ Value}$$

Arithmetic mean/Average return/Mean return: This is also a simple and easy to calculate measure. It can be used for multiple periods. We can use it to calculate average return of different periods (we can use average of holding period returns). Arithmetic mean is upward biased. It means it will give us higher average return if holding periods are not same.

Formula

$$AM = \Sigma\frac{xi}{n}$$

Whereas
AM is Arithmetic mean
Xi is the total return in period i
N is total number of returns

Geometric mean: Geometric mean gives us more accurate results than Arithmetic mean. Geometric mean assumes that the dividend or interest income received in beginning period must be compounded.

$$GM = \sqrt[n]{(1 + X1) * (1 + X2) * (1 + X3) * \ldots\ldots * (1 + Xn)} - 1$$

Whereas
X1 is the rate of return in period 1
X2 is the rate of return in period 2
X3 is the rate of return in period 3
Xn is the rate of return in period n
'n' is the total number of periods

The GM will give us less average than AM.

Internal rate of return (IRR)/ Money weighted rate of return: The simple AM and GM measures are not valid in a complex business and investment environment where there are multiple inflows and outflows of cash. The AM and GM does not consider these occasional inflows and outflows of cash or even initial investment. So in a situation like this, more appropriate measure is IRR.

IRR is the discount rate that makes the net present value of all the cash flows equal to zero.

$$\text{Total value of portfolio} = \frac{Cash\,flow1}{(1+r)^1} + \frac{Cash\,flow2}{(1+r)^2} + \ldots\ldots \frac{Cash\,flow'n}{(1+r)^n}$$

And calculate for r.

Limitations: This method cannot be used when future cash flows are uncertain. Future cash flows are uncertain in case of bonds with embedded options or floating rate bonds. Secondly interest rate risk (changes) is not usually expressed as spread to benchmark. Thirdly the yield is not calculated for bond portfolios. Moreover this method is hard to implement.

Annualized rate of return: Sometimes we have holding period more or less than one year. We can convert it in annual form to compare it with other portfolio`s return.

For example a portfolio has earned 2% return monthly, the annualized rate of return can be calculated as following

Annualized rate of return $= (1 + 0.02)^{12} - 1$

The monthly rate of return must be compounded for 12 months to get annualized return.

If the holding period is more than one year, following method can be used.

For example a portfolio has earned 20% in 24 months, the annualized rate of return can be calculated as;

Annualized rate of return $= (1 + 0.2)^{12/24} - 1$

The 24 months are used in fraction with 12 months.

Other major Return Measures

Gross return: It is the total return on portfolio after the deductions of direct cost or fee. Direct cost or fee is the cost which one must have to pay in order to buy or sell securities like brokerage commission etc. All other fee like management and administration fee are not deducted in order to measure gross return.

Net return: Net return is return after payment of all types of fee.

Pre-tax nominal return: It is the total return before paying any tax (and is not inflation adjusted).

After-tax nominal return: It is the return after paying taxes (and is not inflation adjusted).

Real Return: Return after inflation adjustment. Normally all the returns are quoted in nominal terms. We have to adjust it for inflation. Inflation adjusted returns make the comparison meaningful.

Leverage return: When we use borrowed money, the return on that investment is called leveraged return. In leveraged return we only use the fraction of total investment which is not borrowed. The return on derivatives is also leveraged return because a fraction of underlying asset`s price is deposited (not full price). Use of leverage can boost total return (positively or negatively).

Money-weighted and time-weighted rates of return

Internal rate of return (IRR)/ Money weighted rate of return: The simple AM and GM measures are not valid in a complex business and investment environment where there are multiple inflows and outflows of cash. The AM and GM does not consider these occasional inflows and outflows of cash or even initial investment. So in a situation like this more appropriate measure is IRR.

IRR is the discount rate that makes the net present value of all the cash flows equal to zero.

$$\text{Total value of portfolio} = \frac{Cash\ flow1}{(1+r)^1} + \frac{Cash\ flow2}{(1+r)^2} + \ldots\ldots \frac{Cash\ flow'n}{(1+r)^n}$$

And calculate for r.

<u>*Limitations:*</u> This method cannot be used when future cash flows are uncertain. Future cash flows are uncertain in case of bonds with embedded options or floating rate bonds. Secondly interest rate risk (changes) is not usually expressed as spread to benchmark. Thirdly the yield is not calculated for bond portfolios. Moreover this method is hard to implement. This measure is also very sensitive to inflows and outflows of cash.

Time –weighted rate of return: Geometric means of holding period returns is called time –weighted rate of return.

$$GM = \sqrt[n]{(1 + X1) * (1 + X2) * (1 + X3) * \ldots\ldots * (1 + Xn)} - 1$$

Whereas
X1 is the rate of return in period 1
X2 is the rate of return in period 2
X3 is the rate of return in period 3
Xn is the rate of return in period n
'n' is the total number of periods

Comparison

Money-weighted rate of return is sensitive to the inflows and outflows of cash and their amount. When a manager of a portfolio has full control over inflows and outflows then money-weighted measure is more appropriate. Generally managers do not have control over inflows and outflows of funds.

In time-weighted measure we have different holding periods or we can divide the performance of our portfolio in different holding periods with respect to inflows and outflows of cash. So this measure is not sensitive to inflows/outflows of funds.

Investors always have a choice; they can either choose to invest in lower risk lower return assets or in higher risk with higher return assets. There is always risk-return trade off.

Historic data of USA financial market suggests following

Asset class	Expected average return	Risk (standard deviation)	Liquidity
Large cap stocks	Lower than Small cap stocks	Lower than Small cap stocks	Higher than Small cap stocks
Small cap stocks	Higher than large cap stocks	Higher than large cap stocks	Lower than large cap stocks
Long-term corporate bonds	Lower than Small and large cap stocks	Lower than Small and large cap stocks	Depends on credibility
Long-term government bonds	Lower than	Higher than	Higher

	small cap, large cap stocks and Long-term corporate bonds	Long-term corporate bonds but lower than large and small cap stocks	
Treasury bills	Lower than all above	Lower than all above	Highest than all of above

Mean, variance, and covariance (or correlation) of asset returns

In finance, mean is used to estimate expected return, variance and standard deviation are calculated using mean to measure investment risk while covariance and correlation are used to measure the relationship between two securities.

All these measures are calculated using historical data.

Mean/Arithmetic mean/Average return/Mean return: This is also a simple and easy to calculate measure. It can be used for multiple periods. We can use it to calculate average return of different periods (we can use average of holding period returns). Arithmetic mean is upward biased. It means it will give us higher average return if holding periods are not same.

Formula

$$AM = \Sigma \frac{xi}{n}$$

Whereas
AM is Arithmetic mean
Xi is the total return in period i
N is total number of returns

Variance: It is a measure of dispersion from mean value to calculate risk. A population variance can be calculated as;

$$\text{Variance } (\sigma^2) = \{\sum_{i=1}^{N}(Xi - \mu)^2\} \div N$$

Whereas
σ^2 is population variance
Xi is individual observation
μ is population mean
N is population size.

Sample variance is same as population variance except it is not calculated using whole population (we use a sample size to calculate it).

Sample variance S^2 can be calculated as

$$S^2 = \frac{\left\{ \sum_{i=1}^{n} (Xi - \bar{x})^2 \right\} \div n - 1}{}$$

Whereas;
$\bar{x}$ is sample mean
`n` is sample size

Standard deviation is the "square root of variance"

Covariance: Covariance measures how two variables (expected returns in case of portfolio) move together over time.

Sample covariance can be calculated between two variables x and y as;

$$\sigma x,y = \frac{\sum_{i=1}^{n} (Xi - \bar{x})(Yi - \bar{y})(Xi - \bar{x})}{n - 1}$$

Whereas
Xi is individual observation of variable x

x is mean of x variable values
Yi are individual observations of Y variable
□ is the mean value of Y.
n is the sample size

The value of covariance depends on individual values we use and relationship between variables. A positive covariance means two variables tend to move in same direction. A negative covariance means they tend to move in opposite direction. A Zero covariance means they have no historic relationship. Covariance is an absolute measure and its magnitude does not tell us much. A more standardized measure is correlation.

Correlation: Correlation tells us the strength of relationship between two variables.

Correlation between two variables can be calculated as;

corr(X,Y) = Covariance / σx*σy

σx means standard deviation of x.
σy means standard deviation of y.

+1 correlation means two variables perfectly move in same direction.
-1 correlation means two variables perfectly move in opposite direction.
'0' correlation means two variables are perfectly uncorrelated.

Risk aversion: In portfolio theory it is assumed that the investors are risk averse. They prefer less risky investment over a more risky investment if the outcomes are same or even less. It may also suggest that a risk averse investor gets highest utility when he invests in least risky assets.

Risk seeking: If an investor is risk seeking, it means she love to take risk and prefers more risk over less risk. A gambling behavior is risk seeking behavior. It may also suggest that the risk seeker gets highest utility when he invests in high risk assets with highest expected returns.

Risk neutral: Risk neutral behavior means the investor is indifferent about risk. It may also suggest that the risk neutral investor will get highest utility when he invests in highest return generating security (off course with highest risk).

For example there are two investments with same initial cost but one will definitely generate $ 50 while other can generate $70 inflow or 50$ loss. The risk averse investor will chose the investment which will certainly generate $50 while risk seeker investor tends to chose second investment. A risk neutral can chose any investment (or he can choose second security because it can produce higher return).

Portfolio standard deviation

Let's assume we have two securities (X and Y) in our portfolio. The total risk of our portfolio is not the sum of risks of individual securities as there is covariance involved. Total risk can be less than or maximum equal to sum of individual risks of comprising securities.

Portfolio variance = $(Wx)^2(\sigma x) + (Wy)^2(\sigma Y) + 2WxWy\, \sigma x\, \sigma Y\, \rho xy$

Whereas
Wx is the weight of security X in portfolio
Wy is the weight of security Y in portfolio
σx is the SD of X
σy is the SD of Y
ρxy is the correlation coefficient of X and Y.

Now we know that standard deviation is square root

Portfolio standard deviation $= \sqrt{[(Wx)^2(\sigma x) + (Wy)^2(\sigma Y) + 2WxWy\, \sigma x\, \sigma Y\, \rho xy]}$

σx σY ρxy is the covariance of X ad Y. This result can be derived from following previously used equation

ρ (X,Y) = Covariance / σx*σy

Less than perfect correlation and Portfolio risk

The total risk of our portfolio is not the sum of risks of individual securities as there is covariance involved. Total risk can be less than or maximum equal to sum of individual risks of comprising securities.

If two Securities have -1 correlation (perfectly negative correlation) and their proportion is same in a portfolio, there would be zero investment risk. If one security rises the other will fall with same proportion. If they are perfectly positive correlated (+1correlation coefficient) the total risk is simply the sum of individual risks of each security.

Having a correlation between +1 and -1 is called less than perfect correlation. In this case the overall risk of a portfolio is less than sum of individual risks of each security.

Minimum-variance and efficient frontiers

In finance theory we assume that the investors are risk averse. They do not like risks and want to minimize it. Investors have to find investable securities which are least risky with a given level of expected return. When we make a graph of all these securities, that is called efficient frontier or minimum variance frontier. The portion of efficient frontier where there are least risky portfolios reside is called global minimum-variance portfolio.

To make efficient frontier we select all the securities with minimum variance and given level of return. A rational investor must choose between all those portfolios which are on efficient frontier because they are least risky given the expected return.

All other portfolios or securities are more risky. Note: Here we are ignoring the securities which have zero investment risk (like government issued securities).

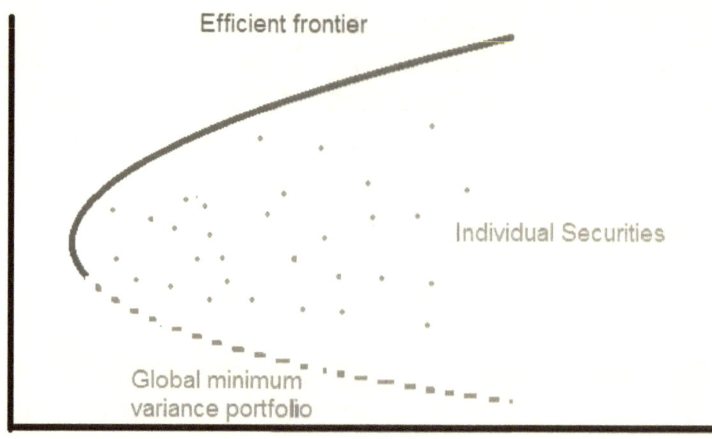

Selection of an optimal portfolio and investor's

Utility: Utility is the quality of anything which can satisfy a human want. In simple words we can say utility is the satisfaction.

Indifference curve: Indifference curve is the combination of all portfolios which gives same level of satisfaction. According to indifference curve approach, utility cannot be measured but we can rank it as higher level of utility and lower level of utility.

Higher Indifference curve (IC) shows higher utility while lower IC shows lower level of utility.

When we combine utility with portfolio management we can express it as follows;

$$U = E(R) - \frac{1}{2}(A\sigma^2)$$

Whereas

U is the utility level of an investment
E(R) is the expected return
A is risk aversion coefficient
σ^2 is portfolio variance

A is the additional reward an investor want in order to accept additional risk so, "A" would be higher for more risk averse investor
"A" would be lower for less risk averse investor
"A" will be zero for risk neutral investor. The utility of risk neutral investor only depends on level of E(R)
And "A" will be negative for risk lover.

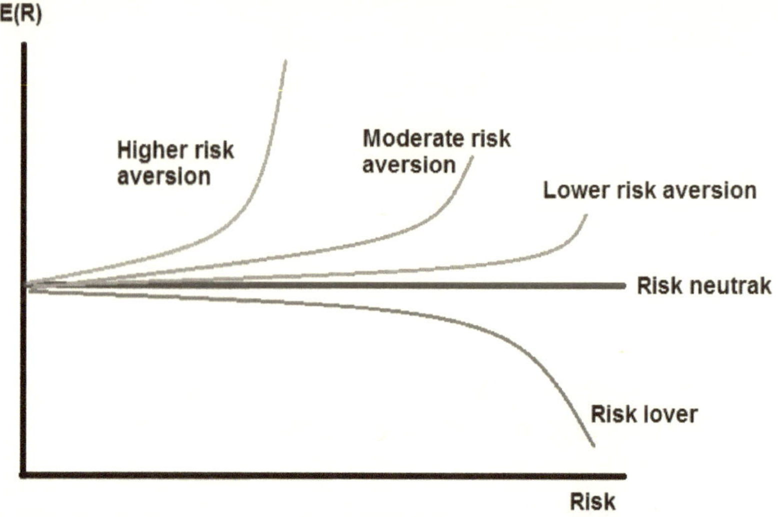

We can see from above figure that, an investor who hates risk has steeper indifference curve because she needs higher reward for one unit of additional risk.

Capital allocation line: The two fund separation theorem states that the optimal portfolio of any investor must have risk free and risky assets.

Capital allocation line shows the risk of risk free assets and risky assets. It is created by combining all possible combinations of risky and risk free assets. It shows the expected return which an investor might earn by assuming certain level of risk. The slope of CAL is the trade-off between risk and return.

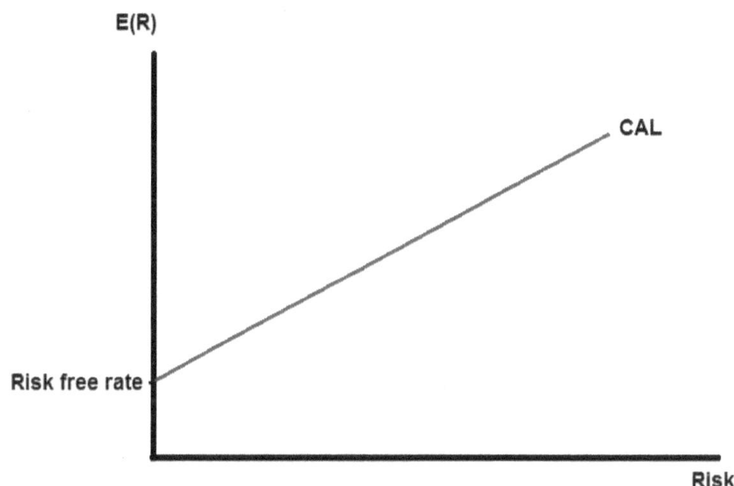

Combining IC and CAL

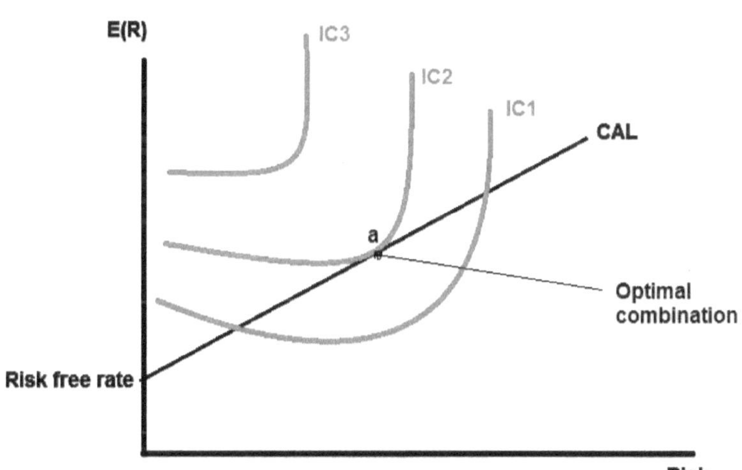

At point "a" of IC2 is the highest level of utility
which an investor can gain given all these ICs
and CAL. IC3 is not attainable while IC1 is not
optimal as the investor can increase her utility

level by going to IC2 and attain extra return with same level of risk.

PORTFOLIO RISK AND RETURN: PART II

Combining risk-free and risky assets

An investor can improve risk and rerun of a portfolio by combining risky and risk-free assets in her portfolio. The expected return of portfolio depends on weights of risk free assets and risky assets in portfolio and their correlation.

If the assets are less than perfectly correlated, the total risk of portfolio is less than their sum of individual risks.

$$E(R_p) = W_{rf}E(R_{rf}) + W_bE(R_b)$$

$E(R_p)$ is the expected return of portfolio
W_{rf} is the weight of risk free asset
$E(R_{rf})$ is the expected return of risk free asset
W_b is the weight of risky asset
$E(R_b)$ is the expected return of risky asset

While the portfolio risk is

Portfolio standard deviation $=\sqrt{[}\ (Wrf)^2(\sigma rf) +$
$(Wb)^2(\sigma b) + 2WrfWb\ \sigma rf\ \sigma b\ \rho rf.b]$

Whereas
σrf σbρrf.b is the covariance of risky and risk free assets.

Capital allocation line (CAL) and the capital market line (CML).

Capital allocation line: The two fund separation theorem states that the optimal portfolio of any investor must have risk free and risky assets.

Capital allocation line shows the risk of risk free assets and risky assets. It is created by combining all possible combinations of risky and risk free assets. It shows the expected return which an investor might earn by assuming certain level of risk. The slope of CAL is the trade-off between risk and return, **(R_p – R_{rf}) /**σ_p (also known as Sharpe ratio).
Rp is portfolio return
Rrf is risk free rate
σp is portfolio standard deviation.
 We will discuss Sharpe ratio in detail later in this book

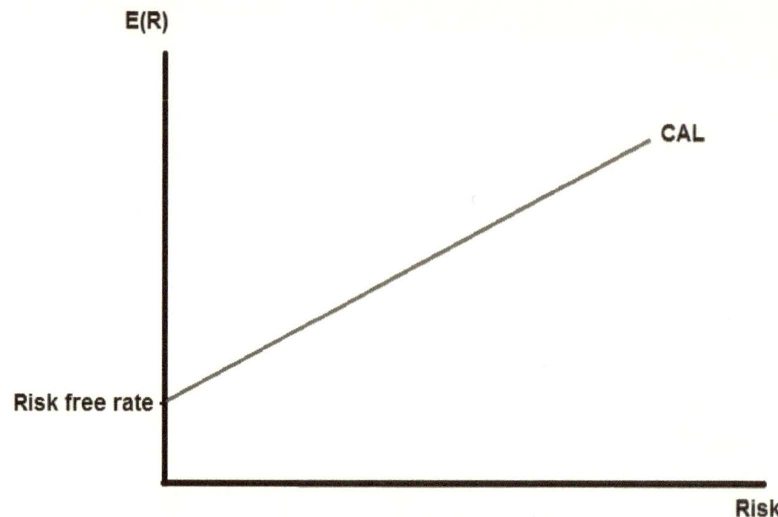

Capital market line (CML): CML is the special case of CAL where the risk-portfolio is the market portfolio.

If for all investors, the expected risk and return characteristics of risk-assets are homogeneous, then all the investors will choose a portfolio of risk-assets on CML which is tangent to efficient frontier.

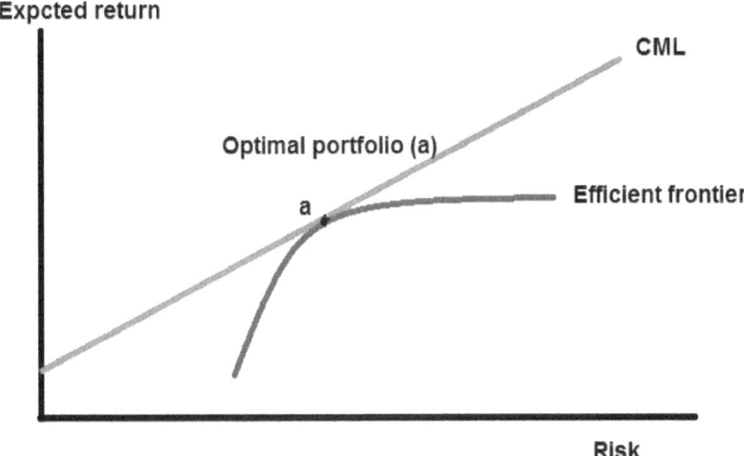

Here optimal risk portfolio is the market portfolio.

In practice, the expected risk and return for all investors is different and they choose different portfolios depending on their risk tolerance and desired return (depend on their IC). Some investors go up alongside of CML or CAL to have higher expected return with extra risk.

Systematic and nonsystematic risk

Nonsystematic risk: The risk attached to a specific security which can be avoided by diversification is called nonsystematic risk. In portfolio theory the nonsystematic risk can be avoided because diversification is free or cost of diversification is extremely low. For example we can hold securities with less perfect correlation or we can buy stocks of a mutual fund which is diversified by professionals.

Systematic or market risk: The risk which exists with the market and cannot be avoided is called systematic or market risk. This risk is attached with the overall market and depends on overall economic variables like GDP growth, interest rate other crisis etc.

Portfolio theory states that as we buy more and more different securities we can diversify our portfolio and the additional risk reduces. Some studies states that holding 30 different stocks reduces nonsystematic risk almost close to zero. So, the investors are only rewarded for taking systematic risk.

Return generating models

Return generating models are used to estimate returns of different securities using different input variables. The most general model which uses almost all affecting variables (like inflation, interest rate, company fundamentals etc) is multifactor model. Multifactor model can be used to estimate the intrinsic value of a single security or a portfolio. The general form of multifactor model is as follows;

$$R_i = E(R_i) + \beta_{i1}F1 + \beta_{i2}F2 + \beta_{i3}F3 \ldots\ldots\ldots\ldots \beta_{in}Fn + \varepsilon$$

Whereas
Ri is the return on asset 'i' or portfolio 'i'.

E(Ri) is the expected return on asset 'i' or portfolio 'i'.

$\beta i1$ is the sensitivity of stock i to the factor 1.

F1 is the first factor that can affect return on asset i.

$\beta i2$ is the sensitivity of stock i to the factor 2

F2 the second factor that can affect return on asset i

βin the sensitivity of stock i to the factor n.

ε is statistical error. It is the return unexplained by any factor.

We can use factors like change in GDP, interest rate, company`s revenues changes etc.

The multifactor model is often expressed in risky minus risk free return as;

$$R_i - R_f = E(R_i) + \beta_{i1}F1 + \beta_{i2}F2 + \beta_{i3}F3 \ldots\ldots\ldots\ldots \beta_{in}Fn + \varepsilon$$

R_f is the risk free rate.

It tells us that the excessive return from risk free rate is dependent on all the factors which we will include in our mode.

Fama and French three factor model: It uses three factors to which expected return is sensitive to. These factors are; Size of firm (small minus big (SMB), Book value to market (high minus low, HML) and excessive return on market portfolio from risk free return ($R_m - R_{rf}$).

$$R_i - R_{rf} = \alpha_i + \beta_{SMB}(SMB) + \beta_{HML}(HML) + \beta_{SMB}(SMB) + \beta_M(R_m - R_{rf}) + \varepsilon$$

This model considers that the small cap value stocks generally outperform the market. This model adjusts the risk factor of these elements.

Single factor model/Single-index model: It is the single factor form of above mentioned model which uses single factor (the market portfolio return).

$$R_i - R_{rf} = \beta_M(R_m - R_{rf}) + \varepsilon$$

Market model:
$$R_i = \alpha_i + \beta_i(R_m - R_{rf}) + \varepsilon$$

Here R_m is the market index return.

Beta

Beta is the risk of a specific security in relation with market risk. Beta is the sensitivity of security`s return to the market index. It measures the systematic risk and its value depends on the correlation between security and the whole market (or index).

$$\beta_i = Cov(R_i, R_m) \div Variance(m)$$

Cov (R_i, R_m) is the covariance of a specific security and market. It tells us how these two move together. A positive covariance tells us

that they move in same direction while negative covariance tells us they move in opposite direction
Variance (m) is the market variance around mean. By definition the beta of market is one so

$\beta i < 1$ it means the security is less risk than market
$\beta i > 1$ it means the security is riskier than market
If Beta is zero it is most likely the risk free security. If the security and the market have no correlation, it can also produce zero beta and that does not necessarily mean the security is a risk free security.
 (We must take absolute values)

A positive beta also means that the security `i` and the market moves in same direction while negative beta shows movement in opposite direction.

Capital asset pricing model (CAPM) and the security market line (SML).

CAPM: CAPM is a widely used model to evaluate the expected return of a security given its risk. It describes relationship between expected return of a security and its systematic risk beta.

CAPM formula

$$E(R_i) = R_{rf} + \beta_i\{E(R_m) - R_{rf}\}$$

$E(R_i)$ is expected return on a security
R_{rf} is risk free rate
β_i is the beta of security i.
$\{E(R_m) - R_{rf}\}$ is the risk premium

Assumptions of CAPM

1. Investors are risk averse. They use diversification to reduce risk.
2. Investors want to maximize their utility. They will choose portfolio according to their utility preferences (on the basis of risk and return characteristics).
3. All the investors have homogeneous expectations about expected return, risk and correlations (that's a very strong assumption)
4. All investors have same time horizons.
5. All investors have free access to all available information

6. The markets are frictionless. It means there are no trading costs, no taxes and no any other restrictions on trading.
7. All securities are infinitely divisible. One investor can invest in any amount of securities.
8. No investor can influence the market.

Security market line (SML): SML is the graphical representation of CAPM. As we use beta in CAPM so in x-axis of SML we have beta for risk (in opposed to CAL where we use total risk on x-axis).

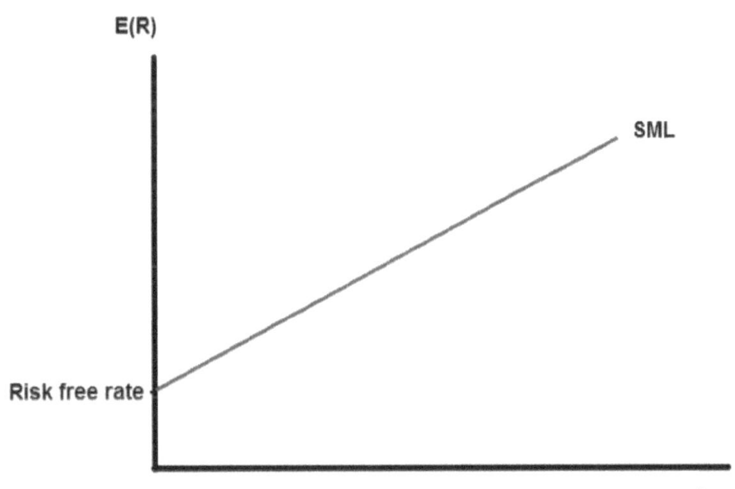

The CAL represents all possible efficient portfolios but SML shows all securities (weather efficient or not). The slope of SML is

{E(Rm) – Rrf} is the risk premium. We know that for efficient portfolio total risk is only the systematic risk.

While
$$\beta i = Cov\ (Ri,\ Rm) \div Variance(m)$$

Applications of the CAPM and the SML

CAPM and SML are widely used for pricing of securities and performance evaluation given its systematic risk. Its calculations are very simple.

Comparison: CAPM can be used to compare risk and return of different securities and an investor can invest intelligently.

This model also helps to construct a diversified portfolio.

With the help of SML we can easily select undervalued securities and sale overvalued securities.

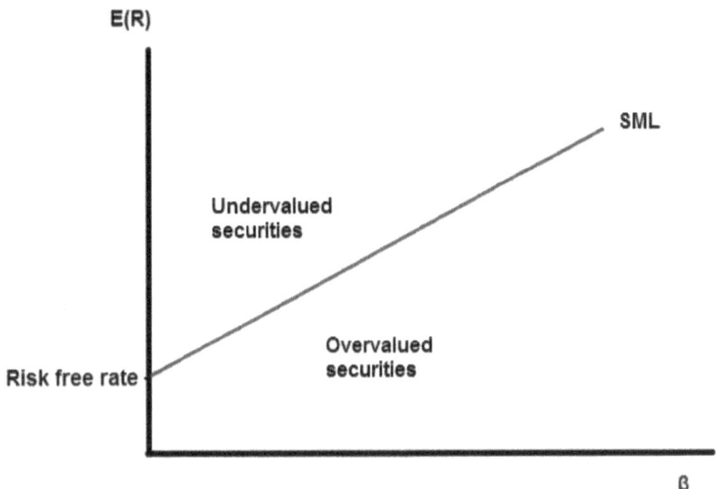

The securities above the SML are undervalued for the given risk and therefore are good buy. The securities under the SML are overvalued and can be sold.

The Sharpe ratio, Treynor ratio, $M2$, and Jensen's alpha.

The sharp ratio, Treynor ratio, M2 and Jensen`s alpha are risk adjusted return measures.
These measures are used to compare different portfolios that have different risks.

Sharpe ratio: Sharpe ratio is the risk premium divided by portfolio risk. Here we use total risk. It is the excessive return per unit of total risk.

Sharpe ratio= $(R_p - R_{rf}) / \sigma_p$

Whereas
R_p is portfolio return
R_{rf} is risk free rate
σ_p is portfolio standard deviation (Total risk).

$(R_p - R_{rf})$ is also called portfolio risk premium.

A portfolio with higher Sharpe ratio is better as it will generate higher risk adjusted returns. Value of Sharpe ratio itself does not tells us anything. It is used to rank different portfolios. Sharpe ratio can help an investor to examine whether the higher returns are due to better investment decisions or due to extra risk exposure.

Limitations of Sharpe ratio: A negative Sharpe ratio either means that the risk free rate is higher than portfolio return or the portfolio is generating negative returns.

Sharpe ratio can also be easily manipulated. The investment manager can use annualized standard deviation or can use standard deviation of most stable period in order to generate higher Sharpe ratio.

Treynor ratio: It is just like Sharpe ratio but we use systematic risk instead of total risk.

Treynor ratio = (Rp – Rrf) / βp

It is the excessive risk on portfolio per unit of systematic risk.

βp is the systematic risk.

A portfolio with higher Treynor ratio is better than another portfolio with lower Treynor ratio because portfolio with higher Treynor ratio will generate better return per unit of systematic risk.
Use of systematic risk is the benefit of this ratio because beta cannot be easily manipulated. Beta also makes more sense as the unsystematic risk can be easily avoided by diversification.
A negative Treynor ratio is meaningless.

Modigliani- Modigliani risk adjusted performance or M-Squared ratio (M^2): It is derived from Sharpe ratio but M^2 gives result in percentage form which is an advantage of this measure.
The intuition behind this measure is that we create a portfolio 'P' that mimics the risk of market or an index.

$$M^2 = (Rp - Rrf)\frac{\sigma m}{\sigma p} - (Rm - Rrf)$$

Rp is the return on our portfolio
Rrf is the risk free rate of return

Rm is the market rate of return

σm is the market standard deviation

σp is the standard deviation of our portfolio

$$\frac{\sigma m}{\sigma p}$$ is the weight of our portfolio in relative to market.

M^2 is also used to rank different investments.
$M^2=0$ means out portfolio will produce market rate of return
$M^2>0$ means our portfolio will outperform the market
$M^2<0$ means our portfolio will generate fewer return compare with the market.

Jensen`s Alpha: It is also a risk adjusted measure. It measures the excessive returns of a portfolio over or below than predicted by CAPM.

Formula

$$\alpha p = Rp - [Rrf + \beta p \ (Rm - Rrf)$$

αp is Jensen`s alpha for our portfolio.

If the Jensen`s alpha is positive, our portfolio have beaten the market (earned more than required rate of return).
If the Jensen`s alpha is negative, out portfolio have not generated the required rate of return and performed poor than market.

If the Jensen`s alpha is zero it might indicate
that our portfolio is perfectly tracking market
or an index and producing same return as the
market is.

BASICS OF PORTFOLIO PLANNING AND CONSTRUCTION

Investment policy statement (IPS)

After examining our (or our client`s) investment goal, time horizon, risk tolerance, liquidity needs, tax and other obligations and circumstances we (the analyst) write IPS (Investment policy statement). IPS contains investment objectives, constraints and a related benchmark to compare portfolio`s performance. This statement can be and should be updated as soon as investor`s (investor can be our client or if we are investing and managing our own assets it means the investor and investment managers are same person) circumstances change. Without writing an IPS the investment manager, we cannot produce high quality results for the client. The IPS is the communication bridge between investment manager and client.

Major components of an IPS

Every client is different, so does their IPS. A Typical IPS has following components;

- Purpose of IPS
- Identifying client`s circumstances, liquidity, tax and other obligations and source of wealth
- Investment objectives
- Risk tolerance
- Client's investment constraints
- Investment time horizon
- Duties and responsibilities of investment manager
- Duties and responsibilities of client
- Client`s familiarity with financial markets
- Special investment guidelines given by client about execution of investment, assets which can and cannot buy
- Procedure of updating IPS
- Evaluation procedure of investment and benchmark
- How to respond in different situations
- Baseline strategic asset allocation rebalancing procedure

Risk and return objectives

Risk and return objectives are most important element of an IPS. The return objectives must be consistent with the risk and investment constraints.

Risk objectives: The risk has two factors; the client's ability and willingness to take risk. If the client has higher (lower) willingness but the ability is low (higher), it should be explained to her. The investment manager and the client must reach at a conclusion. The investment manager must not try to persuade the client to increase or decrease her willingness. If the ability to take risk is not consistent with willingness to take risk, the lower of the two must b considered.

The risk can be stated in absolute or relative terms. The absolute risk can be the probability of total loss like not more than 3% in six months. The relative risk can be attached with a benchmark like LIBOR or any index.

A relative risk can also be attached with the time an obligation will arise like a pension plan.

Return objectives: As stated before the risk and return objective must be consistent. All investors want highest return with zero risk but in practical life this is not possible. According to portfolio theory, if you want more return you must accept higher risk. Return can also be stated in absolute (like 5% p.a) or in relative terms (like track and index).

Willingness and the ability to take risk and financial risk tolerance

The risk has two factors; the client's ability and willingness to take risk.

The ability to take risk is a function of investment time horizon (higher time horizon means more ability), Assets vs obligations (more assets than liabilities means higher ability), having a job or not (having a secured job means more ability), expected future income (higher income means higher ability) etc.

Willingness to take risk is a function of client's attitude and believes about investment. Willingness is a very subjective term and the investment manager must take good care in judging it.

The willingness and ability to take risk must match.

If the client has higher (lower) willingness but the ability is low (higher), it should be explained to her. The investment manager and the client must reach at a conclusion. However, the investment manager must not try to persuade the client to increase or decrease to her willingness. If the ability to take risk is not consistent with willingness to take risk, the lower of the two must b considered.

Investment constraints and their implications for the choice of portfolio assets

Liquidity constraints: Liquidity constraints are essential part of IPS.
Different investors/clients have different liquidity requirement at different point in time. Individual investors might have to pay for their child's college fee or to purchase a house in future. In addition to this there are several unpredicted liquidity needs like medical expenditures.

Institutional investors like insurance companies need cash to honor mostly unpredicted claims. The pension plans have mostly predicted cash needs.

The investment manager must carefully consider the liquidity requirement of the client and plan the investment accordingly. A bond can be held in portfolio maturing at same time when the cash is required is generally a good strategy.

For unpredicted liquidity requirement most liquid assets should be included in the portfolio. The hedge funds and private equity which is very illiquid investment should be avoided for high liquidity requirement.

Time horizon: Time horizon must be included in IPS. If the time horizon of an investor is short, the manager must not invest in risky assets. For longer time horizons (all other things held constant) the investment can be made in riskier and illiquid assets.

Tax concerns: The tax treatment for different investments is different. Sometimes the capital gain tax is higher than dividend or interest income. On some investments the tax can be deferred. A taxpaying investor may want to invest in tax free investments (like government securities) or in dividend paying securities. Tax concerns must also be included in IPS.

Legal and regulatory factors: Legal factors are also included in IPS. There are some general rules of financial markets. In addition to these rules there are several restrictions for individual investors. For example director of a company face restrictions to invest in his company as he may has inside information about that company. These legal and regulatory factors must be considered by investment manager.

Unique circumstances: There can be some unique investment circumstances for some investors. For example some investors do not want to invest in tobacco or alcohol providing firms. Some investors prefer not to invest in a company whose main business is on interest basis. These unique circumstances must be included in IPS.

Asset classes and asset allocation

Broadly, the cash, equity, bonds and real estate are considered major asset classes. All these asset classes are traditional investments. A recent trend about investment also includes alternative investment like hedge funds, private equity, Real estate investment trusts, art etc.

All these asset classes can be subdivided into many other groups with respect to their category. For example equities can be divided with respect to issuer's size (large, small) or its geographical location (domestic company or foreign company), market liquidity (small cap or large cap), multinational or local, service sector or manufacturing sector etc. The bonds can be grouped as government bonds or

corporate bonds, investable or junk bonds.
There are many other ways by which these
broad categories can be further divided.

After writing objectives, constraints and other
circumstance in IPS we develop strategic
allocation of investment in different asset
classes according to liquidity needs, legal and
tax circumstances, risk and return requirement
etc. The correlation within an asset class must
be high positive to ensure that the assets
belong to each other. While the correlation
between different asset classes must be low for
diversification.

Principles of portfolio construction and asset allocation

After the creation of IPS and strategic
allocation of assets have decided, the
investment manager constructs the portfolio
according to the investment objectives and risk
tolerance of the investor on the efficient
frontier.
While constructing the portfolio the investment
manager considers the utility of investor.
Utility of investor increases with increase in
expected return with appropriate risk.

The investment manager (by the approval of
investor) can choose tactical allocation (active

management with short term deviation from the strategic allocation of assets) or passive management (strategic asset allocation) or a mix of both.

In *tactical asset allocation* the managers try to exploit a short term opportunity of earning extra return from mispriced securities which is may or may not consistent with the investment risk and return objectives.

Security selection: The investment manager try to select the securities within asset class which are best matching the investment objectives and their expected returns are higher than benchmark.

After some intervals (or when the situation changes) the portfolio should be rebalanced.

There are two famous strategies in portfolio construction; top-down approach and core-satellite approach.

In *top-down approach* many investment managers of same asset class work for the single client and mange risk. This approach generates average total return and reduces the biasness of a single manager. As they can be following same benchmark, the risk budget may be underutilized. Moreover there would be higher trading cost (due to frequent trades) and tax obligations (due to capital gains).

The core- satellite approach come up with a better solution. In this approach, major investment is made in passive management while a small portion of total investment is actively managed. The tax obligations and cost due to frequent trading can be reduced with this approach.

ESG integration and portfolio planning

ESG integration: While making investment decisions in companies, the investors consider these companies' impact on environment, society and governance. The responsible and cautious investors avoid all those companies which are affecting negatively (to EGG). This practice is called ESG integration into portfolio planning and construction.

ESG can be divided into following sub-categories;

Environmental issues: Like increase in pollution, contaminating water etc.

Social issues: Like child labor, gender inequality etc.

Governance issues: Like bribery, corruption etc.

For example avoiding investment in tobacco companies is a common practice.

The investors set some criteria and eliminate all those companies from the list who are using 'bad practices'. This can limit their investable asset and their overall returns might be reduces. The research on ESG and return suggests mixed results.

RISK MANAGEMENT

Risk management

Risk can be defined in a single word as 'uncertainty'. When the future outcome of an investment is not 100 percent certain it is called risky investment. Almost a certain level of risk is involved to all of our activities including investment. The individual investors and institutions can reduce the risk that is called risk management.

The institutes can reduce the risk by identifying the risk, calculating their risk tolerance, choosing which and how much risk they can take and transferring the risk to another party (i.e. insurance companies).

Individuals can also reduce the risk by not investing in junk securities, diversifying and using insurance products.

All those process to reduce the risk is called risk management.

Features of a risk management framework

Every organization faces risk especially the firms in investment industry. Actually firms benefit from risk because without risk there is no reward. The firms create a framework to manage risk so they can balance the risk and return. Effective risk management increases the credibility of firms, giving them more access to low cost capital. Investors do prefer the firms that have effective risk management framework.

A good risk management framework must have following features;

- A process to identify risk
- Process and policies for risk governance
- Risk measurement and risk tolerance of the firm
- Minimizing risk
- Reporting and monitoring of risk

Risk governance

It is a top to down process. The governing body of a firm defines risk goals of the firm and identifies the risk tolerance. They risk management team decides which risks they can take, the risks they can reduces and the risks they should be avoiding. Then a process is established to ensure that each and every employee is performing his/her duties in consistent to risk management framework. The role of employees is defined and authorities are assigned to monitor and for approvals of different employees actions.

Risk tolerance and risk management

As we know that every firm has to take a certain level of risk in order to achieve its goals. The risk tolerance is the firm`s ability to withstand in case of losses. The firm can face internal as well external risks.

The risk tolerance can be a function of

- The firm`s ability to respond a certain bad event
- Firm`s ability to stay undamaged in losses
- Firm`s competitive environment
- Regulatory environment

The risk management team can determine types of risk the firm can take, can be reduced and those which should be avoided, in determining the risk tolerance of the firm. Only those risks should be accepted which give better reward and are consistent with firm`s goals.

Risk budgeting and its role

After determining risk tolerance there comes risk budgeting. In risk budgeting we allocate all of our investment in different assets. The aggregate risk of these assets must be equal to our risk tolerance level. In this way we choose all those investable assets which give us maximum return within our risk budget.

We can budget our risk using a single measure or by using multi-dimensional measures

Following are the most common single measure being used for portfolio risk budgeting;

- Standard deviation
- Downside standard deviation
- Value at risk
- Beta

- Portfolio duration

For multi-dimensional measures, factor analysis is most common. In factor analysis, different factors (interest rate, exchange rate etc) are analyzed how much they can affect different asset classes.

Some common risk budgeting practices are

Limit the beta to 0.90

Allocate 90% of portfolio in government securities and 10% in corporate bonds

Allocate the investment in those assets which can be least affected by interest rate change.

Financial and non-financial sources of risk

Financial risks are related to financial market like unfavorable market movement or share price movement. Non-financial risks are risks which are not related to financial market. The source of non-financial risk can be within an organization or outside of the organization (but not from the financial market).

Financial Risks

Market risk: The unfavorable movement of share price, a downfall of overall market, changes in interest rate etc.

Credit risk: Risk of default of counterparty.

Liquidity risk: The risk that the firm will not be able to sell an asset at a fair price. This usually happens in a stressful market or when the underlying asset has less liquid market.

Non-financial risks

Legal risk: Risk that counterparty will sue you.

Compliance risk: Risk that an organization will not meet the regulatory requirement. This also involves un-ability to meet recent changes in taxation laws, accounting disclosure requirement etc.

Model risk: Risk of using un-appropriate model for security evaluation.

Tail risk: Risk that an extreme event will occur which will affect the organization in a bad way. The returns on financial markets do not follow normal distribution. There are usually "fat tails".

Solvency risk: Risk that the company will be defaulted.

Operational risk: The risk that the employees of an organization can make errors which can cost the organization.

Political risk: Risk that the government`s policies will change.

All these risks interact with each other. The total risk might be bigger than the sum of all these risks.

For example, suppose a big customer failed to pay the services he has taken from the organization. Due to a customer`s default, our firm may not have enough cash to pay its suppliers and employees. Some employees can be fired which sued the firm and there is legal risk.

Measuring and modifying risk exposures

Most common risk measures are as follows;

Standard deviation: It measures the volatility of returns. It is most common measure of risk when the distribution of returns is normal. In financial markets the outcomes do not generally show normal distribution. This measure is not good for negatively skewed or fat tailed distributions.

Beta: It measures the systematic or market risk. This measure assumes diversification so it is good for portfolio.

Duration: It measures the sensitivity of debt securities (fixed income) to change in interest rate.

Value at risk (VaR): It measures the risk of loss on an investment. It tells us minimum losses over a specific period with a given probability in normal business conditions. This method is being widely used by investment and commercial banks.
 For example an investment firm has VaR of $2 million with a probability of 1% in a week. It

means that the chances of losing $2million in a week are 2%.

<u>Drawbacks of VaR:</u> It does not tell us maximum losses.
It uses normal distribution which is the rare case in financial markets.
It can be manipulated by using most stable periods.
Critics claim that VaR usually understate the actual situation.

Due to all above drawbacks VaR should be used along with other risk measures.

We have a better modified value at risk model called

Conditional value at risk (CVaR): Also called expected shortfall. It uses the weighted average of tails of a distribution. Due to this the CVaR goes beyond the VaR. It is more conservative approach to measure the value at risk.
When the expected outcomes are stable, the normal VaR is sufficient. But with more volatile expected outcomes, we need to use CVaR.

The derivative risk measures

They are also called "the Greeks". They are used to measure the derivative risks.

Delta (Δ): It is the value sensitivity of a derivative to change in the price of underlying asset.

Δ = Change in price of derivative ÷ Change in price of underlying asset

For example if Δ for an option is 0.5, it means if the price of underlying moves by $1 the option price will change by $0.5 in same direction (due to positive sign of delta).

Theta (θ): It tells us how much the value of an option will fall as the time to expiration decreases. Theta is expressed as daily decline in value and its value is generally negative.

Gamma (Γ): It is the rate of change in Delta if the price of underlying asset changes. Higher Gamma shows higher sensitivity of derivative to its underlying.

Vega: It measures the rate of change in price of derivative in response to change in volatility of underlying asset.

Rho: It tells us the rate of change in derivative price when the interest rate changes.

Subjective risk measures

Scenario analysis: In scenario analysis we use different scenarios and see what can happen to our portfolio in those scenarios. Scenario analysis does not tell us a single Value but different outcomes under different scenarios.

For example we can see what worst can happen to our investment if the interest rate increases along with exchange rate movement.

Stress testing: In stress testing we take extreme cases (like market crisis etc) and see what will happen to our investment.

Modifying risk

Modifying risk does not necessarily means avoiding the risk. It means rebalancing the risk. Some risks can be accepted while others can be reduced and avoided.

The goal of risk modification is taking optimal level of risks.

Risks can be avoided by not taking part in those activities. If the expected returns of a security are highly volatile, the investor can avoid it. The securities which have crossed a border line of a certain level of risk can be reduced from a portfolio and the other securities of fewer risk characteristics can be added.

Some risks can be prevented. For example operational and compliance risks can be prevented by enforcing strong procedures and systems.

Some risks must be accepted to achieve organization`s goals like investment risk.

Some risks can be transferred to insurance companies.

Risks can also be shifted. Shifting can be done by the use of hedging in derivative market.

Choosing a modification method

The method of risk modification should be adopted by considering cost-benefit analysis. Usually the companies use a mix of differ modification methods.

For example banks heavily depend on insurances but they also use hedging.

TECHNICAL ANALYSIS

Technical analysis: It is a practice of using past prices and volumes to predict future prices of securities (to value securities) in a free market.

Assumptions of technical analysis

- Technical analysis assumes that the market prices solely depend on demand and supply.
- Supply and demand in the market depends on rational and irrational factors. Irrational factors include mood, guess, belief etc. Actually the technical analysts emphasizes that the market trends heavily depend on human mood and guessing (not on rational basis).
- Individual prices of securities follow the market trends.
- All historical trends repeat themselves over and over again.

Major difference between technical analysis and fundamental analysis

Fundamental analysis focuses on long term strategy. It uses the data from financial statements and tries to find out the intrinsic value of a company. The fundamental analysis assumes that the markets are efficient and they quickly adjust to new information.

On the other hand the technical analysis is a short term strategy. It uses the historical trends and volumes to predict future price of a security. It assumes that the markets do not adjust quickly as there are always information gap between investors. The new information does not come in the market abruptly. The market adjusts gradually.

Implications of technical analysis

- The technical analysis is easy to use. The technical analysis uses different types of charts and tries to predict future.
- The inputs of this analysis are historical data which is the actual data and not the estimates.
- The historical data may not be a valid predictor of future
- There are other factors which influence the security prices but are not considered in technical analysis.

Technical analysis charts and interpretation

Technical analysts are called technicians. They use historical data of prices and volumes to create charts. They use these charts to predict future trends. There are different types of charts used by technicians.

Line chart: These are the most common charts used in technical analysis. A line chart or graph shows different prices (or volumes) of a security in different times. We usually take closing prices. On x-axis we have time while on y-axis we use price or volumes. The original values or log of values are used in plotting the points. A typical line chart looks like this

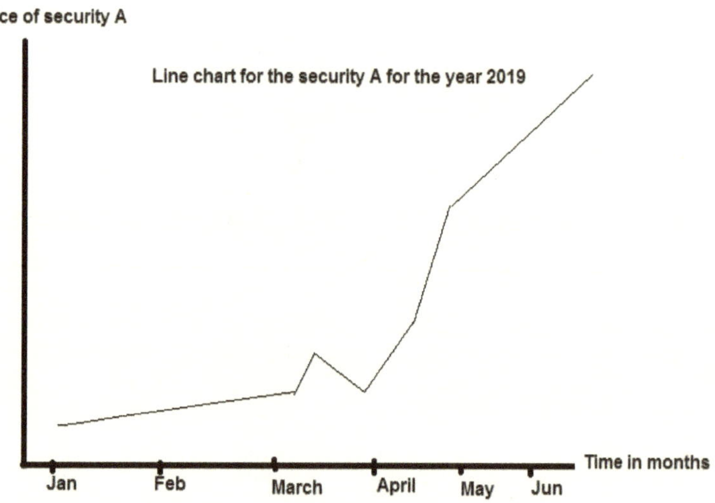

Bar chart: A bar chart has four points; the opening price, closing price, high price and low price. Bar charts usually display daily data but can be used for months too. It shows daily sentiments of the market.

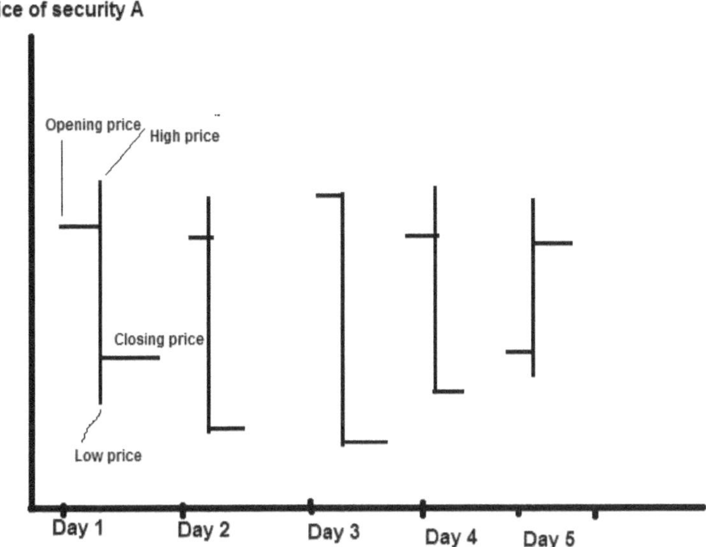

Candlestick chart: It is just like bar chart. It also has four points; the opening price, closing price, high price and low price. One difference between bar and candlestick chart is the candlestick charts are either hollow or shaded.

A shaded candle shows that the closing price is lower than the opening price. A hallow candle shows that closing price is higher than the opening price.

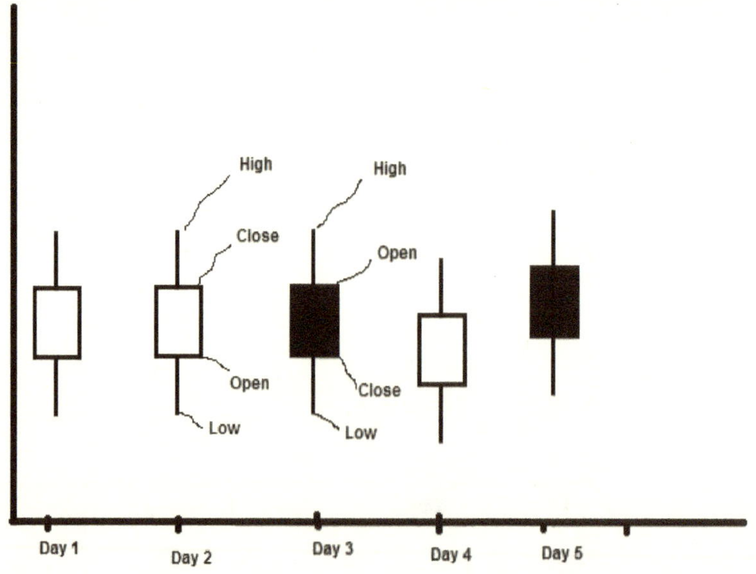

Point and Figure chart (P&F chart):

This chart is different from the other charts. The Xs and Os are created. The Xs shows upward movement of price by a set of amount (called box size) while Os are created for downward movement of prices by a set of amount (called box size).

The box size depends on the price of security and investor`s preference.

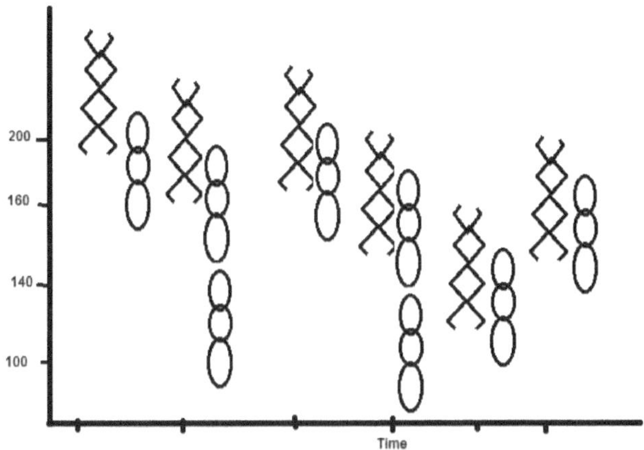

Trend, support, resistance lines, and change in polarity

Trend: Trend is most common thing in technical analysis. It is the direction of movement of the market or a specific security. Generally all the investors on aggregate follow a trend in a market.

Uptrend: It is the upward movement of prices. The graph makes new higher heights and higher lows. This happens due to high demand and lower supply. The users of technical analysis want to buy and hold for some time to profit from this trend.

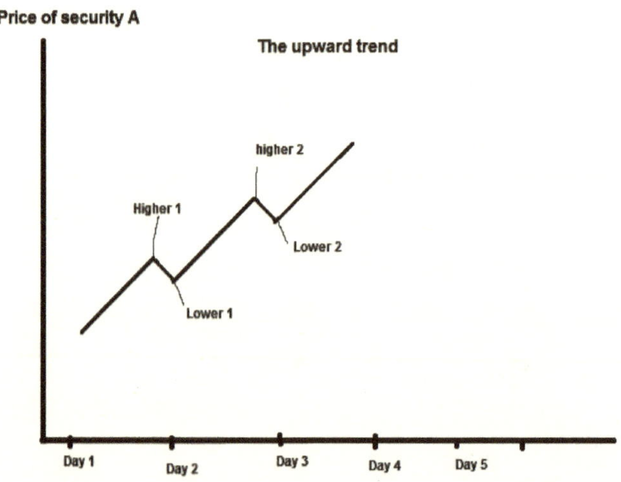

<u>Downward trend:</u> A trend with lower peaks and lower lows is called downward trend. This happens due to lower demand and higher supply. The followers of technical analysis sale their positions even short sell to buy at lower rate.

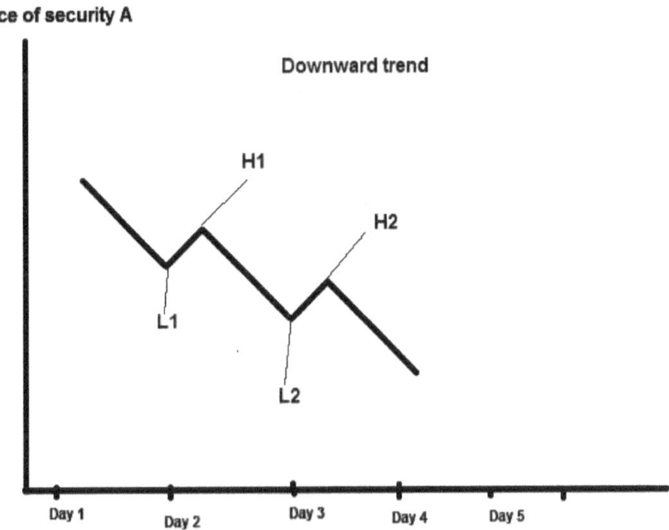

Support and resistance

Support: It is the lower price range at which the technicians think that the price will not fall further because investors will start buying at that level.

Resistance: it is the higher price range at which the technicians believe there would be more selling and the price will not go up further.

The support and resistance levels involve investors' trading habit and psychology.

Change in Polarity: It means once a support level is breached (the price moved beyond level) that support becomes new resistance and if the resistance is breached that becomes new support.

Common chart patterns

There are two major chart patterns; the reversal and continuation patterns. One thing to remember first, there is always market noise in formation of these patterns. They do not look clearly like the following graphs. These graphs show the general picture.

Reversal pattern: It indicates that the prior pattern tends to reverse once the pattern is complete. If there is previously uptrend (or downtrend) the future trend is going to be downward (or uptrend).

In order to predict the future, the pattern must be clear. Following are some famous reversal patterns;

Head and shoulder patterns: It looks like one head and two shoulders. It comprises of a higher peak (the head) and two lower peaks (the shoulders).

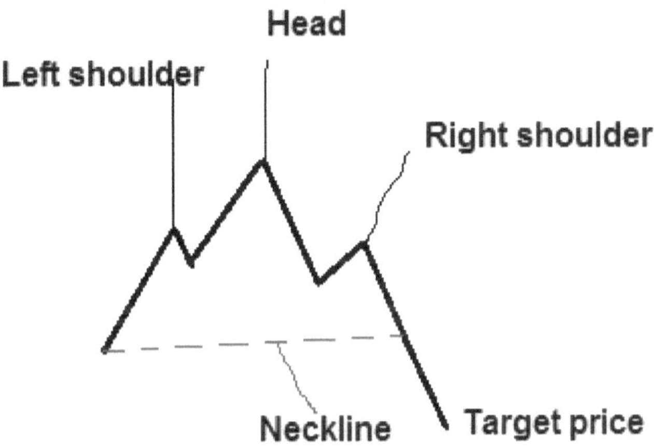

An investor should wait until the pattern completes itself. A semi complete pattern is not enough and the future price movement may not create the pattern at all.

Once the pattern is complete wait for the penetration in neckline. Once the neckline is penetrated that's the target price to buy. After buying, the target sale price can be any shoulder price or the head. Targeting the head for sale is too risky because it may not be achievable.

Inverse Head and shoulder pattern: It the opposite of head and shoulder pattern. It is a downtrend.

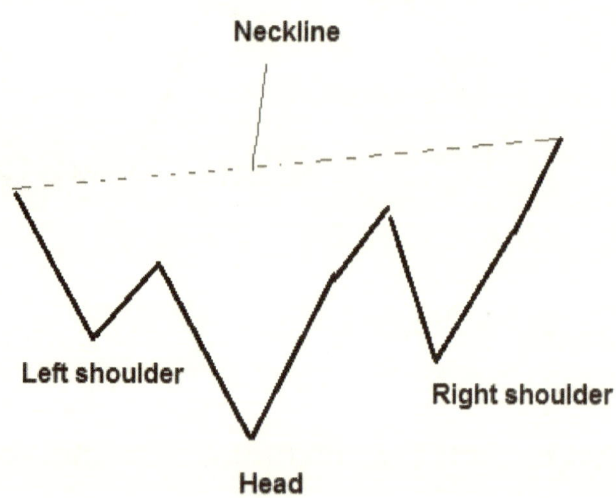

Double top or triple top pattern: When a security tests the resistance level two times or three times but could not penetrate then it moves downward. Its shows downward trend in future once the pattern is complete.

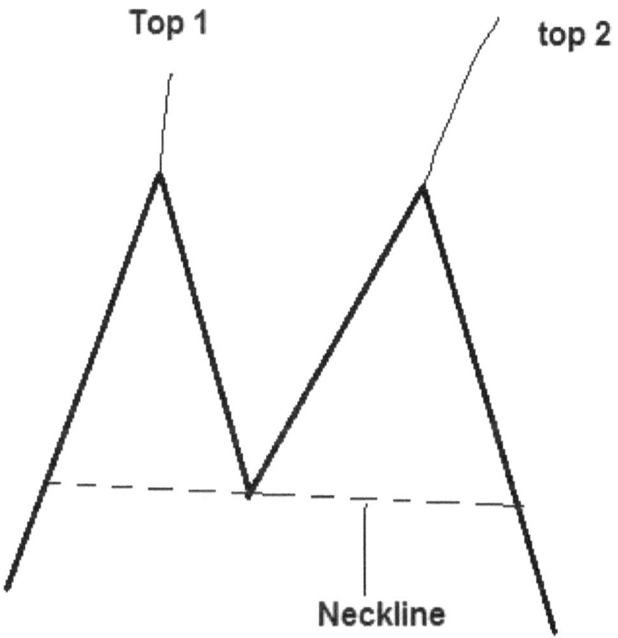

Double or triple bottom: Inverse of double or triple top.

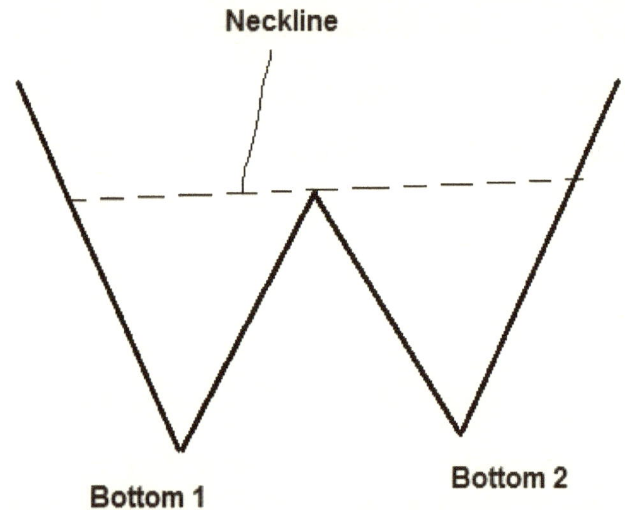

The security price has tested the support level twice or thrice but could not go beyond and go back. This is an upward trend in future.

Continuation pattern: These patterns show that the prior trend will resume once the pattern is complete.

Following are the patterns in continuation pattern; ascending triangle, descending triangle, symmetrical and rectangle formation.

Ascending triangle: Two or more highs form a horizontal line. The higher points show that the price is getting resistance at that level. But if the graph shows higher lows, the price may break that resistance level (bullish).

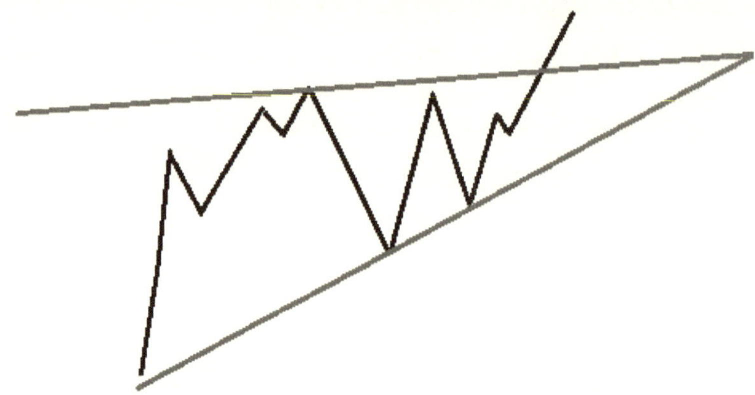

Descending triangle: It is a bearish formation and shows downward trend. Two are more lows form the bottom line of the triangle. At the lows, the security is getting support and does not cross that level. If the highs are getting low it shows the bearish trend and once the resistance level crossed, the price may move downward.

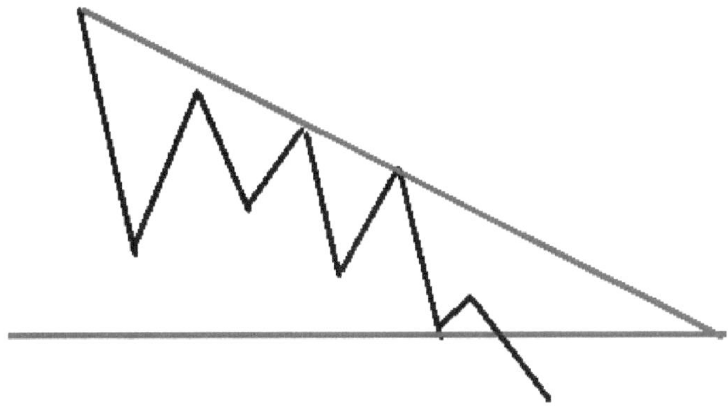

Symmetrical triangles: Two or more lower highs and two or more high lowers form symmetrical formation. The price may move up or down after this pattern.

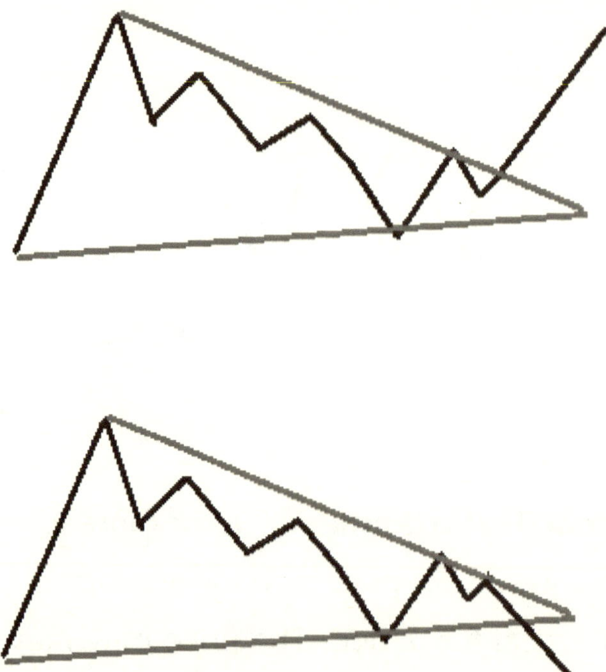

Rectangle pattern: Two or more same highs and two or more same lows. It shows when the price moves up to a resistance level then the investors start to sell and the price falls but after touching support level investors start buying and the price goes up. It's a rare but simple formation.

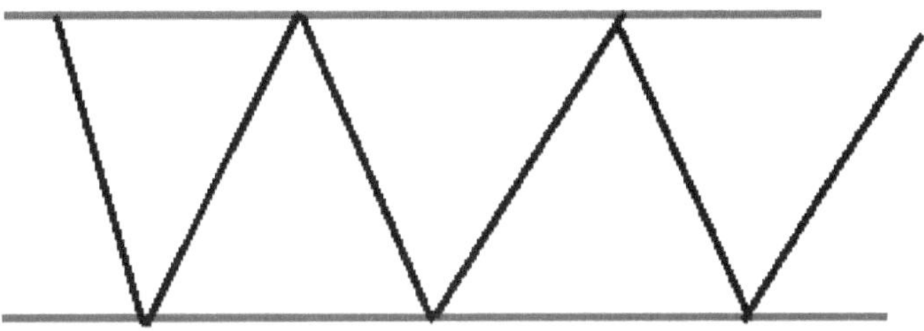

These are four common technical analysis indicators which try to predict future of market prices.

Price-based indicators: Price based indicators use historical and current prices to predict future prices. Common price based indicators are;

Moving Average/Rolling mean/Moving mean: It is the average of last n number of prices (usually we take closing prices). It is the average of a specific amount of data over a time period. Moving average is good measure to analyze the trends because it smoothes out the prices and excludes the short term market noise. For example moving average of last 30 days prices or last 60 days prices can give us a clear picture of current trends in the market.

Golden cross: Golden cross is short term moving average like one week moving average or last 14 days moving average. It gives us information about current bearish or bullish trends.

Bollinger bands: It is the standard deviation of last n number of prices (closing prices). It indicates the price deviation from mean (moving average) in last n number of days. It is usually represented in a graph which shows upper line and lower line. The upper and lower lines are the extreme deviations from the mean. A narrow Bollinger band is good.

Momentum Oscillators: It measures the rate of change in security price.

$$M = (P_t \div P_0)100$$

M is the momentum

P_t is the current price

P_0 is the price in some previous time like one week ago.

If the momentum oscillator is less than 100, the prices are falling. When the values are more than 100 the prices are rising.

The followers of technicians start buying when the momentum is less than 100 (and or is at historical lowest point) because it indicates the oversold security and it will bounce back. On the other hand, when momentum is greater than 100 people start to sell because the prices will move back.

Some technicians use following formula for the momentum oscillator instead of above;

$$M = (P_t - P_0)100$$

In this case the negative momentum is our less than 100 momentum (previously used) and a positive momentum is greater than 100.

Moving average convergence-divergence (MACD): It indicates a bearish or bullish market and their strength.

MACD= 26-period Exponential Moving Average (EMA) - 12-period EMA.

We use exponential moving average (instead of simple moving average) because it gives more weight to current prices.

Relative strength index (RSI): It measures the speed of price change.

$$RSI = 100 - \frac{100}{1 + (average\ gain \div average\ loss)}$$

The value of RSI remains between 0 and 100. Typically when the value of RSI is above 70 it means the security is over overbought. When it falls below 30 it is considered as oversold.

Stochastic oscillator: Stochastic means point of current price in relative to its range of prices over some period of time. Its values can move between zero and 100. It is overbought or oversold indicator.

Formula

$$\%k = \left(\frac{Current\ closing\ price - Lowest\ price\ in\ last\ period}{Highest\ price\ in\ last\ period - Lowest\ price\ in\ last\ period}\right)100$$

The value of stochastic oscillator near 20 means the prices are near its lower point in a given period while the value of this oscillator 80 or above indicates that the prices are near upper price range.

Sentiment indicators: These indicators are used to measure the investors` sentiments about the market. These indicators are graphical as well as numerical. Following are some common sentiment indicators;

- Market Vane Bullish Consensus
- Investment Intelligence Advisors Sentiment
- Daily Sentiment Index
- New York Stock Exchange (NYSE) High/Low Indicator
- Odd-Lot Trading Statistics
- CBOE Volatility Index (VIX)

The analysts gather data and try to establish a relationship between these sentiments and prices.

Flow of funds indicators: These indicators measure the inflow and outflow of funds in the market.

Common indicators here are

Arms index: Also called short term trading index (TRIN).

Arms index =

$$\frac{\dfrac{number\ of\ stocks\ with\ rising\ prices}{number\ of\ stocks\ that\ are\ decling\ in\ prices}}{\dfrac{Number\ of\ stocks\ that\ are\ advancing\ in\ volume}{Number\ of\ stocks\ that\ are\ decling\ in}}$$

Arms index =1 means the market is balanced

Arms index <1 means more money is going in rising stocks and the trade is getting bigger.

Arms index >1 means more trade is taking place in falling stocks.

Mutual fund cash position: Mutual funds hold some cash for investment and other needs (up to around 12%). More cash ratio (more than 12%) may indicate that the market is going down (Bearish). It may also means that the managers of mutual funds are holding cash and waiting for good time to invest. Ultimately they have to invest and the market will move up.

IPOs: It tells us number of new IPOs. If the number is going up, the prices may fall and vice versa.

Technical analysts and market cycles

Cycles are the fluctuations in prices that repeat again and again. Technicians use these cycles to predict the prices.

Presidential cycle: It is believed that in USA, after the election and selection of president the first one to two years are bad for the financial market and it goes down. Following years are of economic boost when the president seeks for re-electing. In this period the policies are business favorable and the market improves.

The 18-year cycle: This cycle is especially for real estate sector but it may affect other sectors too. There is a short term recession in mid of every 18 years and longer term recession at the end of18 years.

The decimal pattern: It is believed that market performance can be attached with the last digit of a year. In a year with zero at the end like 2020 the market will perform extremely poor and in a year ending at digit 5 the market performs great.

Elliott Wave Theory

Ralph Elliot in 1930s developed this theory. This theory is against efficient market theory or hypothesis. Ralph Elliot revealed that the chaotic financial market movements are actually following two patterns; Motive wave and corrective wave.

According to this theory these two moves are repetitive. The motive movement is in same existing direction while a corrective wave is against existing direction.

The corrective wave movement of the market is against overbought and oversold situations.

He argued that these waves actually depict the investors` psychology.

One thing to note here is this theory does not tells us the future with certainty but it suggests general trend and should be used along with other technical analysis tools.

This theory seconds the Fibonacci numbers because Fibonacci sequence repeats itself in Elliot wave structures.

Key tenets of the theory:

The wave cycle completes in 5-3 move.

Five motive movements are followed by three corrections.

The 5-3 pattern remains constant however the time period for each may changes.

Inter market analysis

Inter-market analysis is the comparison between one asset class with another asset class and one financial market with another financial market. The purpose of this analysis is to determine which asset class or market is performing better than other.

The asset classes my include equity stocks, bonds real estate or subdivisions of these classes.

The analysis of different financial markets may include a comparison between NYSE with London Stock Exchange etc.

The inter market analysis helps the investors to choose wisely and optimize their investments. They can allocate their investment in better performing asset classes in better performing markets.

FINTECH IN INVESTMENT MANAGEMENT

FINTECH

Innovations, development and use of new technology in investment industry are called Fintech (means finance and technology).

 Due to fintech now the investors and managers can invest their money and manage portfolios from home. The new bank accounts and insurance products can be purchased and sold from anywhere in the world through internet and computers. Investors can buy and sale option contracts by using their fingers.

The huge amount of data and graphs can be analyzed using computer software and the investment decisions can be made quickly to exploit any opportunity. Due to fintech markets are also performing more efficiently and adjust to new information within seconds. The liquidity problems are extremely low.

Due to fintech the new products are evolving in the financial markets quickly. These new products are solving a large number of problems which were only a dream before technology.

Fintech is also being used in auto record keeping, examining "big data" auto investment guidance (robo-advisors), risk management and auto execution of orders.

Big Data, artificial intelligence, and machine learning

Big data: "Big data" include huge amount of traditional and non-traditional data to analyzed, predict patterns and trends about the future of financial market movement. The big data can include

Traditional data sources like

- Financial markets
- Company`s financial statements
- Macroeconomic and statistical variables

Non-traditional data sources like

- Bank records,
- Other Financial institutions
- Radio
- Television
- Social media
- Individuals
- Mobile phones

Artificial Intelligence: It is the use of machines to perform financial tasks intelligently. By intelligently means machines are using cognitive and decision making abilities. When the machines perform these tasks, they can do it at a very fast pace in comparison to human being. The "intelligent" machines use what-if and other complex mathematical structures in these tasks.

Machine learning: Machine learning is a part of Artificial intelligence. It is referred as programming the machines so they can learn by themselves. The data can be inserted in machines and let them make models, recognize patterns and give us the outputs. Machine learning can be divided into supervised learning and unsupervised learning.

Supervised learning: In this type of learning the inputs and desired outputs are inserted (labeled data) in the machines and let them model the data (also called labeled training).

Unsupervised learning: In unsupervised leaning the data is not labeled and let the machines to structure the data with common characteristics.

Distributed ledger technology

Distributed ledger: Unlike central recording authority, distributed ledger is a database shared on a network. Each participant can update entries in the database and all the participants have identical copies of the ledger. The system is placed to ensure that only authorized participants (also called nodes) can update and record the entry.

When one node makes an entry other nodes verify that entry. If the majority of participants (nodes) agreed then the new entry is recorded.

Distributed ledger can be permission-less and permission-able.

In permission-able network all the users have different level of access for example some can add the transaction, other can see the history of transaction.

In permission-less network all the participants can see the transaction. One thing to remember here is no one can change the historical transactions.

Benefits of distributed ledger:

Cryptography: Distributed ledgers use cryptography. The cryptography ensures that the unauthorized persons cannot use or change it. For this reason the distributed ledgers are considered more secure and reliable.

Smart contracts: These are the self executable electronic contracts which are programmed to perform certain tasks when certain conditions are fulfilled by counterparties. For example in derivatives, if one party defaults, the underlying asset can be automatically transferred to other party.

Tokenization: It is an electronic proof of ownership of assets. It replaces the paper proof of ownership. The electronic proof is visible to all parties and can be easily verified.

Crypto currencies: Most of the crypto currencies use distributed ledger technology. All the investments and payments can be made in this currency.

The companies can raise capital by initial public coin offerings (traditionally IPOs).

Crypto currencies are latest phenomena and most of the central banks do not allow the use of these currencies because these currencies do not involve central monetary authorities (central banks).

Post-trade clearing and settlement:
Through distributed ledger technology, trades can be verified automatically and quickly and the clearing and settlement can be done with great ease.

That's all for the portfolio management. Dear reader if you feel any problem do not hesitate to contact us at

Whats app# 00923465006818

Ch.ImranAhsen@gmail.com